Self-Hypnosis Techniques:
Learn Self-Hypnosis Using Scripts

Shanna J. Levitt

This publication is designed to provide accurate and
authoritative information in regard to the subject
matter covered. It is sold the understanding that the
publisher is not engaged in rendering medical
services. If medical advice or other expert assistance
is required, the services of a competent professional
person should be sought.

First Printing, 2011

ISBN: 978-1460962947

Printed in the United States of America

Dedication

To those who
want to get beyond
"you're getting very sleepy…"

Table of Contents

Part 1:

Introduction to Hypnosis

Chapter 1

Understanding Hypnosis

For many people, the word "hypnosis" conjures images of mysterious men with swinging pendulums, holding innocent individuals under their sway.

You would often read or hear of people saying, *"Never look into a hypnotist's eyes!"* – as if hypnotists have magic of their own and anyone can fall into their complete control, like robots.

Popular culture hasn't helped clear the air of such misconceptions and fallacies. There have been countless movies depicting hypnosis as a means to gain an unfair amount of control over a person's subconscious.

Since you are reading this book, we are going to assume that at some point in time, you have been curious as to what hypnosis really is and how it works.

This book will cover these topics – and more. The main goal of this book is to allow anyone to *use* self-hypnosis to improve parts of their lives that may have been neglected for some time. Hypnosis is not a magical tool – nor is it a weapon to wield against people.

From our perspective, self-hypnosis is primarily a tool for self-improvement and health enhancement.

Thanks to modern medical science, hypnosis has been acknowledged as a valid alternative health practice for more than fifty years now.

What practitioners knew about the subject back in the day are still applicable today, but we are much more fortunate now because we have been able to refine the existing hypnosis techniques so anyone can apply it specifically to improve one's self.

Let us clarify the nature of hypnosis, so you can better understand why it is one of the most natural occurrences in the world.

Hypnosis is actually a *heightened state of concentration* where a person is able to give almost one hundred percent attention to a particular stream of thoughts.

This heightened state of concentration happens when we watch television (which is why the media is so powerful), or when parents teach impressionable children life lessons.

As a person ages and matures mentally, the process of hypnosis becomes more and more complicated because the person already has many normative values that are supported by both the subconscious thought processes and the *conscious,* or waking, thought processes.

That's why hypnosis was born as an independent discipline - because in order to be utilized properly, there should be a well thought-out process. The end result of *any* hypnotic effort is *self-hypnosis.*

Anyone can be hypnotized. But the effectiveness of a hypnosis technique varies from person to person, depending on the person's desire to accept the hypnosis process.

If a person consciously resists hypnosis, then the effectiveness of the method is reduced drastically. That's why the belief that hypnotist's eyes can control people is completely wrong. It has no scientific bearing and has no rational basis at all.

Chapter 2

History of Hypnosis

Hypnosis has been known to man for thousands of years. Historically, the practice of altering man's consciousness has been carried out by shamans, Wiccans, spirit mediums, and spiritual doctors, for various reasons.

Ancient civilizations of Egypt and Greece recorded that the fastest way to get in touch with the spiritual realm is through rituals that are similar to what are now called hypnosis, meditation, visualization, and drugs.

Experiences common to deep sleep, anesthesia and the power of the subconscious have been noted in different religious documents, such as in the Old Testament of Christianity and in the Talmud of Judaism.

Some accounts even say that many women were accused as witches and thus burned at the stake because of their practice of "cutting up" women's bellies during difficult labor in order to help the child get out of the womb.
I
It was said the mothers felt relatively no pain during the "operation" and the babies were delivered successfully – with the midwives using only herbs and oils while uttering some comforting, soothing chant.

This practice, many believed, is one of the earliest known practice of what is now called delivery through Caesarean operation, with the aid of hypnosis.

Taking the cue from their ancient traditions, indigenous cultures even in the present day, still take benefit from mind control and suggestion its ability to heal – or harm.

Mesmerizing Magnetism

In the modern world, hypnotism's first brush with science was known in the late 1700s, through Austrian physician Dr. Franz Anton Mesmer and the "phenomenon" that was called animal magnetism. Mesmer believed that through a mystical force channeled through water tubs and magnetic wands flowing from him to his subjects, he could make people and animals go under trances.

He claimed this mystical power was due to magnetic waves. He lulled his subjects into submission through fixating them on a certain object, and through monotonous repetition of certain words. This was where the word "mesmerize," which we still use today to pertain to the act of being in awe and dumbstruck to a certain figure, was coined.

But soon in the further scientific study of hypnotism, the concept of animal magnetism was eventually dismissed. Abbe Faria, a scientist in the 19th century, declared that the hypnotism practiced

by Mesmer was not because of animal magnetism –
but through the power of suggestion.

The Pendulum

More studies and experiments in mind
control followed through the years, but it was a
research launched in 1842 that was considered the
turning point in the study of Mesmer's ideas.

Scottish surgeon James Braid was one of the
first scientists to attribute the process of going under
a trance to a physiological process.

He believed that the state of trance was not
due to the magnetic power of the hypnotist; but
through hard, rapt attention on a striking, moving
object over time, as in that iconic clock necklace.
"Protracted ocular fixation," Braid believed, will
make the brain tired and will cause the subject to be
under what he called "nervous sleep." Thus Braid
coined the term "hypnotism" and "hypnosis," based
on the Greek word of "sleep."

Braid, with his contemporaries such as
Ambroise-Auguste Liebeault, Hippolyte Bernheim
and J.M. Charcot, later focused more on the impact
of psychological motivation in hypnosis rather that
their early concept of fatigue and nervous sleep.
They were also the first ones to tread upon medical
hypnosis, wherein they used hypnotism to treat
different psychological and physical conditions.

Following the paths taken by Braid et al., more studies on the use of hypnosis in medicine followed – with better results this time. Mirroring (though perhaps unconsciously) the practices of ancient doctors, modern medicine started to cautiously tread upon the use of hypnosis as anaesthesia or pain killers.

The medicine world then had a strong disbelief in this method; as in a case in 1842, when there was a report of a successful and painless amputation procedure through hypnotism. But it was quickly dismissed.

Still, pro-hypnotism medical professionals persisted with their studies. Dr. James Esdaille, a British physician who practiced in India, performed almost 400 pain-controlled operations with patients under hypnosis.

Known as the "Father of Hypno-anesthesia," Esdaille also integrated his Western education with the culture in India. Hand-in hand with his medical practice, he also performed a drugless trance therapy traditionally from Bengal, India.

Esdaille's cases listed eye, ear, and throat operations, amputations, and tumors and cancerous growth removals. Esdaille reported no pain and zero mortality under his so-called "mental anesthesia."

What's more astonishing is that after the surgeries, Esdaille further hypnotically suggested to his patients that their wounds would not result in any kind of infection or side effect. True enough, no one among his patients was reported to have caught any post-operation side effects.

Many believed the subconscious aspects of Esdaille's subjects responded well to hypnotism. When Esdaille suggested they would not be infected, their bodily functions acted accordingly and launched antibodies that would fight infection.

Soon, the death of Braid, Esdaille and other kindred colleagues, plus the advancement of anesthetics though chemicals, waned the interest in hypnotism.

Hypnotically Hysterical

Hysteria and hypnosis? Strange bedfellows at first glance maybe; but after hypnosis kept a relatively low profile after Braid, hypnotism made a comeback in the 1880s as new versions of his work were circulated.

The revival also came with new experimentations, particularly in the use of hypnosis in treating hysteria led by neurologist Jean Martin Charcot.

Charcot, and later his pupil Pierre Janet, treated various cases of mental conditions, but most particularly hysteria, through what they called *dissociation*. This technique, utilized in a big number of patients, compartmentalizes some of the data stored in the mind, so that aspects such as a particular skill or information from the past can be hidden or retrieved.

Considered landmark experiments at that time, these findings impressed and inspired later works of French psychologist Alfred Biet and the father of psychoanalysis Sigmund Frued

In fact, Freud used the works of Charot and another French doctor, Hippolyte Bernheim, to strengthen the framework of his initial studies on the unconscious and hypnotism.

Meanwhile, science has enriched layman's dictionary once again since it was in this time that Ambroise-Auguste Liebault coined the term *rapport* – meaning that critical and required consensus between the hypnotist and the subject for a successful hypnosis session.

Today, we still use the word rapport to mean that pleasant communication connection between two parties, a certain similarity in wavelength.

Hypnotism and War

A powerful weapon, a strategic device, an intelligence technique and a medical tool – all these roles were said to have been taken by hypnosis during World Wars I and II.

War trauma is common to soldiers who have faced the horrors of war. Hypnotism was used by physicians to help patients in letting go of their repressed memories, and to eventually treat amnesia or other resulting conditions.

This kind of therapy also helps the patient alleviate emotional and mental tensions resulting from the trauma.

The powerful suggestion invoked by hypnosis was also used as a tool for military intelligence.

For example, extremely confidential information that has to be passed personally can be protected through the power of suggestion. In this case, the information will be given to a soldier under hypnosis.

After the information has been relayed successfully, the hypnotist then suggests to the courier that he will never remember a single detail about the message, thus ensuring that it remains a secret forever.

Since hypnosis can also be effective in altering the behavior of a person, it was used as a strategy to infiltrate the enemy's ranks.

G.H. Estabrooks, a physician who has worked with United States Authorities in World War II, divulges in a medical journal that the behavior modification properties of hypnosis were useful in sending a deep penetration agent inside a communist territory.

He also narrated: "I worked this technique with a vulnerable Marine lieutenant I'll call Jones. Under the watchful eye of Marine Intelligence I spilt his personality into Jones A and Jones B. Jones A, once a "normal" working Marine, became entirely different.

He talked communist doctrine and meant it. He was welcomed enthusiastically by communist cells, was deliberately given a dishonorable discharge by the Corps (which was in on the plot) and became a card-carrying party member."

Chapter 3

Hypnosis for Regression

Hypnosis may not make you younger, but it can make you feel and act younger. It may not take away pain, but it may fool around with your pain sensors so that pain may virtually be nonexistent.

For all the fallacies and myths surrounding hypnotism, there are still a number of things hypnosis can do that are beneficial and scientifically proven.

In general medicine, psychology, surgery and dentistry, and even in the legal system, hypnosis has been known to help people gain better understanding of the situation and themselves.

Age Regression

Wise men have said: "Those who do not remember history are condemned to repeat it. Whatever you are now, the skills you possess, the ailments that bother you, may have something to do with your past."

In regression, the person that initiates your hypnotism dips into a particular period in your life – say, when you were still in kindergarten. This suggestion triggers you to seem to live out significant incidents in that period.

Since you are "re-living the past," it will relatively occur that you think, talk, or act as you were in kindergarten.

Your therapist and you can then determine how a particular incident in that particular period may have connection with a condition affecting you presently.

Reliving a part of your past may help you recover some vital information, establish insights, or aid you to know yourself better and how to cope with the present.

Past Life Regression

Stretching the theory further, some have claimed regression can make them go into the past deeper – and can let them experience their lives when they were in the womb.

Still an area of contention, more so because this theory touches on religion, the concept of a past life or reincarnation is relative to a person's faith.

Scientifically, it is not possible, as scientists say that the brain is still underdeveloped during pre-natal stages to store memories.

Still, thousands of cases have been documented of people going back to their past lives. These people were convinced because they found accurate connections between their past and present identities.

In age regression, it is believed that getting to know what you were in the past may help you understand and eventually cure a certain condition. A stereotype case would be, for example, a woman who is afraid of going near bodies of water may have died due to drowning in her past life.

Tool for Surgery

Painless surgery and dentistry has been proven to be possible with just the help of hypnosis.

Probably the most natural form of anesthesia, mothers about to give birth, soldiers wounded in the midst of a battle, or children nervous about a tooth extraction – have benefited from hypnosis as an anesthetic.

During the operation, the hypnotized patient is reported to have remained relaxed and at ease. Post-surgery hypnosis is also known to aid in prevention of infection or to relieve discomfort or post-surgery pain.

Increased recovery speed is also a known benefit of hypnosis.

In one case study, a research by a psychologist, states: "In one case, doctors had to graft skin onto a patient's badly damaged foot. First, skin from the person's abdomen was grafted onto his arm. Then the graft was transferred to his foot. With hypnosis, the patient held his arm tightly in position over his abdomen for three weeks, then over his foot for four weeks. Even though these positions were unusual, the patient at no time felt uncomfortable."

Behavior Modification

Making someone act like a chicken is only icing on hypnosis' cake. There are other pleasant and useful cases wherein its ability to modify behavior is vital.

Mental patients who are disturbed or nervous may be helped to be calm through hypnosis, rather than experiencing the side effects of sedatives or be forced into submission through a straitjacket.

On a long–term basis, hypnosis can then be used as a central part of treating psychological conditions such as anxiety, depression, trauma, or phobias.

Long-term therapy with the aid of hypnosis is also required in curbing problem habits such as smoking, drugs, eating disorders, or dilemmas in socialization.

Treating Physical Problems due to Psychological Factors

A lot of our physical problems are linked with our psychological condition, given the direct link of the brain and the nervous system to the separate processes of the other parts of the body.

That's why some doctors believe there is no other way to treat a physical condition more efficiently than to go directly to the brain.

Psycho-physiological conditions are ailments of the body that can be rooted from psychological factors.

Usually, a person vulnerable to a certain illness, when faced with stress, will likely catch a psychosomatic illness.

A medical definition usually states that a psychosomatic illness is a condition in which the state of mind (psyche) either causes or mediates a condition of actual, measurable damage in the body (soma).

Columbia Encyclopedia further notes a psychosomatic disorder as an "emotional disturbance that is manifested as a physical disorder," such as childhood asthma, ulcers, hypertension, endocrine disturbances, and possibly even heart disease.

In most cases the illness occurs only when both physiological predisposition and psychological stress are present.

In this formula, predisposition pertains to your mental and medical history. Stress concerns with elements that make you feel anxious or bothered, as well as outside stimuli such as problems in the family or society, eventually triggers the onset of illness. These include death, conflicts (personal or social), emotional problems, and financial worries.

Other conditions that result from psychological stress are problems that affect vital organs: the heart, stomach, lungs, liver and the nervous system, triggering the onset of cancer, stroke, arthritis, multiple sclerosis and pain.

A typical script when using hypnosis as a form of aiding the treatment of psychosomatic illnesses is similar to other hypnosis techniques that aim at changing or asserting a certain condition.

First, the hypnotist guides the subject into deep relaxation – until the body and mind are completely at ease. The patient is then encouraged to imagine each and every part of his personality that is ailing – physically and mentally.

Using visual imagery that promotes well being and lightness, the hypnotist tells the patient to ease away his pain, anxiety, and other thoughts that bother him. The hypnotist may also identify each body part, giving particular importance to the affected ones, and helps the patient handle, overcome, or come to terms with the pain.

Legal Aid

The mind's capacity to store information is astounding. It can even act like a video camera that zooms in, pauses, fast forwards or slow motions a certain event.

The problem is, we tend to "forget" because however big its capacity, it is not limitless; it compartmentalizes and organizes memory so it can accommodate more. This is where hypnotism comes in.

Hypnosis helps a person to archive and retrieve relevant information that may have been discarded or neglected in normal everyday activities.

Pinpointing critical data is especially important in solving crime cases. Hypnosis has been used to help witnesses and victims of crime sort out information from the crime scene.

By intensely focusing through hypnosis on memories relating to the crime, a significant detail, a vital clue, or an element previously looked upon may aid in the investigation.

Still, police do not usually rely heavily on hypnosis in solving crimes. The mind is tricky, and people can be tricky too. As we said before, people under hypnosis can still decide for themselves. People under hypnosis may lie, or prefer not to divulge a secret.

Chapter 4

Hypnosis as Therapy

Strictly speaking, hypnosis cannot be used to cure any medical condition. Essentially, hypnosis is drug-free therapy that can be used to:

1. Improve a person's ability to manage stress.

2. Reduce anxiety and excessive worrying.

3. Progressively develop self-confidence.

4. Control negative or destructive habits.

5. Overcome shyness.

6. Improving sleep & resolving insomnia.

7. Developing creativity and talents.

8. Memory improvement.

9. Improve focus (for study or work).

10. Improve a person's organizational skills.

11. Facilitate progressive relaxation.

12. Increase reflexive responses.

13. Improve a person's ability to manage all types of pain (including chronic pain).

14. Increase one's motivation to accomplish tasks for work and study.

15. Help slow down premature aging.

16. Alter and improve a waning career path.

17. Help manage grief and loss.

18. Hypnosis can also be used as an alternative therapy for tension and migraine headaches.

19. Fight any kind of phobia – including phobias that have existed for years.

20. Physical problems like chronic allergic reactions and poor immunity can also be addressed and remedied with hypnotherapy.

21. Create harmony and balance in the mind and body.

22. Therapy for OCD or obsessive-compulsive disorders

How Hypnosis Works

As we have mentioned earlier, hypnosis capitalizes on a person's ability to focus closely on a specific thought – but unlike what humans normally do, hypnosis forces one to temporarily loosen one's hold on *rational consciousness* so the subconscious thought process can be accessed.

This is done to introduce new thoughts and concepts to the subconscious, which holds the invisible reins that control rational thought processes.

The subconscious provides the initial impetus to do something and the *conscious* part of our thinking provides the willpower. Without willpower, any big changes to a person's way of living or way of thinking are impossible.

Until very recently, people still thought of hypnosis as a potentially dangerous technique that could be used to exert control over unwilling individuals.

It's time to unlearn this image of hypnosis – because people actually spend 75% of their whole lives in a state of *hypnosis,* or heightened focus.

Because the subconscious is in charge of shaping a person's personality and emotional drives, it is more effective in accepting new suggestions than a person's waking consciousness.

Hypnosis techniques usually involve five distinct components:

1. Complete relaxation of the subject.

2. Heightened concentration on phrases, ideas or suggestions.

3. Subject becomes immobile during the hypnosis.

4. All five senses are heightened during the hypnosis. This is called hyperawareness. It happens naturally when a person increases his concentration during a state of complete relaxation.

5. REM or rapid eye movement can also take place when a person is hypnotized.

There are also two different ways that a person can accomplish self-hypnosis:

1. **Autohypnosis** – this type of hypnosis is achieved by a lone individual, without the help of a hypnotherapist or guide.

2. **Heterohypnosis** – this is a type of hypnosis that requires the help of a guide or a professional hypnotherapist.

Now, we should note that self-hypnosis, or hypnosis *without* the help of an active agent or external force, is actually a *skill*.

This being the case, it should be studied at least over a short period of time. This book focuses on reducing the learning curve by focusing on the most important components *before* introducing actual techniques.

Some of you may be wondering – why would anyone want to go to a professional hypnotherapist if self-hypnosis is possible through autohypnosis?

Well, professional hypnotherapists are adept in *preparing* a person for hypnosis as well as creating the appropriate setting for the hypnosis to take place.

The effectiveness of the hypnosis is completely up to the person who wishes to be hypnotized. According to doctors, hypnosis can be likened to being slightly inebriated.

This might sound like an awkward comparison, but what doctors are pointing out is that when a person has imbibed a small amount of alcohol, he is more open in communicating and is also more open to *accepting* suggestions.

The Power of the Subconscious

The human mind can be viewed as being composed of two major halves – the conscious half and the subconscious half. Though some theoreticians propose a more complex model, for the purpose of self-hypnosis, this particular model of the human mind is sufficient to get our point across.

Now, many people think that rational thinking is more powerful than the subconscious, because it's the type of consciousness that we are more familiar with and we tend to think that logic 'controls' the subconscious.

In reality, what we do in the waking world (with the help of logical consciousness) is actually dictated by our subconscious drives. That's why many people say that they do certain things because of what they have been taught when they were young.

In many ways, the subconscious half of the human mind serves as the control center for normative teaching.

And normative practices are very powerful – so powerful in fact, that when a person becomes *accustomed* to something (say, smoking) the rational half of the mind cannot immediately take control of the activity or habit.

Now, knowing that subconscious drives take precedence over conscious rational drives, if you want to alter something deep-rooted (like a lack of self-confidence), the best route is to implant suggestions directly into your subconscious thinking instead of relying on your waking consciousness - which is, in fact, only *reflecting* what lies "hidden" in the subconscious thought processes.

The following table provides a direct comparison of waking consciousness and the subconscious:

Type of Consciousness	Characteristics
Waking consciousness	• Logical • Actively differentiates rational thoughts & irrational thoughts • Critical • Regularly analyzes situations in everyday life • Where natural willpower manifests • Systematic • Structured • Utilizes common thought patterns & routines • Learning is accomplished through repetitive practice
The subconscious	• Provides simple responses to input • Does not directly utilize logic or rationalization • Core of habitual activities (which is passed on to waking consciousness) • Childlike

How Willpower Is Formed

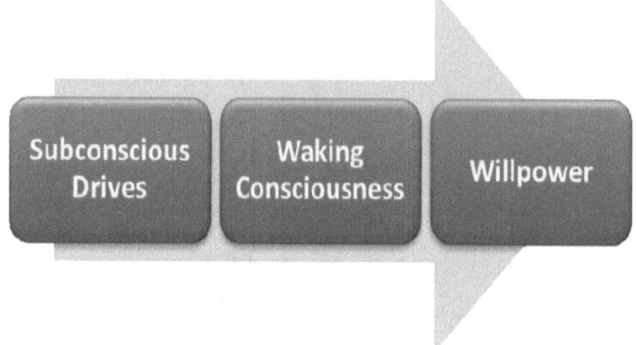

This diagram illustrates the chain that gives rise to a person's willpower or natural willingness to think or act in a particular manner.

Despite the strong dependency of the waking consciousness on the subconscious, the two halves of the human mind are *distinct* and *separate*.

Due to this separation, it is difficult to change subconscious drives *through* the waking consciousness because that is not how these emotional and behavioral drives are formed and perpetuated by the human mind.

The subconscious is fully capable of making changes to the way a person thinks when he is in his waking consciousness. But that doesn't mean that the waking consciousness can easily change whatever is deeply rooted in the subconscious. On the contrary, the logic of the waking consciousness is *not* the language of the subconscious.

Some people might argue: I do most of my thinking when my consciousness is fully awake. I also tend to dismiss irrational thoughts, so how come my subconscious is suddenly so important right now?

Well, the waking consciousness might have a larger role in logical tasks and learning, but it's your subconscious that shapes the following:

- General behavior

- Outlook in life

- Emotional balance

- Emotional expressiveness

- Social preferences (e.g. people you prefer to mix with, etc.)

- Big & small habits

- Romantic preferences

Consciousness Weight Scale

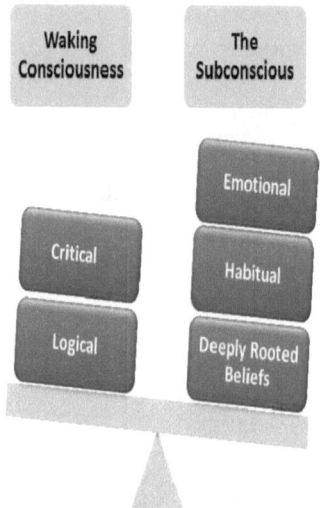

In the final analysis, the subconscious' role in shaping your life is has more weight than your waking consciousness' role.

Now, while a lot of people might not have been focusing on these aspects of their life, it doesn't mean that these components are not important.

On the contrary, these components of the human personality dictate whether or not a person will be able to achieve his goals in life.

These unconscious drives also have a large bearing on the way a person builds health and wealth. The *means* to acquire health and wealth are also dictated by the various subconscious tools or drives that a person has acquired over the years.

What hypnosis does is to go straight into the subconscious half of the mind and *reprogram* aspects of this half. For example, some people have been trained subconsciously to be loners and to shun a healthy social life. You would be hard-pressed to convince a person who has been a loner for thirty years to suddenly change his ways simply because such change is perceived as positive.

The Thought Ladder

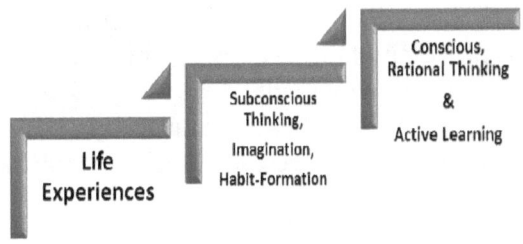

Life experiences are processed first by the subconscious half of the human mind, before rationalization & logical thinking comes in at the last phase of learning & permanent knowledge acquisition.

For many years there has been an effort to create a viable connection to the subconscious through the use of the waking consciousness. These methods of psychotherapy have been proven to be laborious.

In fact, people would exert less effort through hypnosis since hypnosis targets the subconscious *directly* instead of trying to appeal to it through waking consciousness.

If we were to view the human mind as a computer (which it is – a super-efficient organic computer), hypnosis can be seen as *active programming*.

Socialization and learning are forms of active programming that make use of *waking consciousness*. That's why when we study, there has to be some structure or system, otherwise, knowledge acquisition would not be possible.

While *learning* is easy, *un-learning* bad habits and negative thinking requires a bit more effort – self-therapy, if you will. Hypnosis is essentially *intervention* or *change* that capitalizes on the human imagination – the source of a person's brilliance and creativity.

Hypnosis achieves this by implanting suggestions or individual ideas into the subconscious. When this input (the hypnotic suggestion) is introduced, the subconscious part of the human mind processes the new suggestion and prepares the waking consciousness to make the new suggestion a complete reality.

Chapter 5

Entering a Trance

A *trance* is a state of consciousness where a person heightens his focus or concentration on a single idea or a *series* of ideas. The term *trance* is usually associated with the practice of hypnotherapy – but hypnotherapy is *not* the only avenue where a natural trance can occur.

A trance can occur when:

1. A person becomes completely engrossed in reading a book.

2. A person focuses intently on a story being played on television.

3. A person listens to a particular type of music, repeatedly, every day.

4. A person listens to another person who is in a position of authority or power (*e.g.* your boss, a team leader, a professor, a child listening to a parent, etc.).

5. A person engages in daydreaming.

In addition to ordinary activities, a natural state of trance or altered consciousness can also be achieved through the following:

1. Physical activities that require repetitive movement & rhythm, such as dancing and exercising.

2. Chanting

3. Progressive meditation

4. Praying

All types of rituals (may involve just one individual or a group of individuals; the effect would be the same for just one person or for numerous members of a participating group).

Many people are afraid of actively entering a trance because popular culture has depicted trances as potential weapons against free will.

The part that people often miss about trances is that *free will is not suspended* during hypnotic trances. You are free to accept or reject hypnotic suggestions *during* the actual trance.

What To Expect During Hypnosis

Hypnotherapists make use of a variety of tools and techniques to achieve the desired goals. Such results may include positive habit formation, unlearning of bad habits, stopping substance abuse, and implanting positive ideas.

Expert hypnotherapists are quite adept in achieving complete relaxation in individual patients or subjects. Suggestions or commands are given to make the hypnotic session more effective, and in the beginning, you may become very open to hypnotic suggestions.

But this does not mean that you will not be able to resist any or all of the hypnotic suggestions. *Suggestion control,* or the ability to resist hypnotic suggestions, is another skill that can be developed and honed through time. The more you attend hypnotherapy sessions, the more this skill will be refined.

Now, despite what the majority of people may think about hypnosis, the person must possess two things to make the hypnosis effective and truly meaningful to their life:

1. The genuine desire to make a change in their life.

2. Real motivation to achieve the end-goal of the hypnosis.

The second part of this book will provide self-hypnosis exercises that you can try at home. Note that *before* you can effectively utilize these exercises, you must first deal with *underlying resistance.* Underlying resistance are issues that you may have that may directly affect your ability to change a habit or improve your mental state.

Now, what do people *feel* when they are subjected to hypnosis techniques for the very first time?

Some people are disappointed, since the experience is not as 'extreme' as what they had thought at first. Many people think that undergoing hypnosis means falling half-asleep. Some expect that they would feel like floating, with the hypnotherapist's voice being their only guide back to the real world.

Some people might experience these things, but for the most part, people say that a hypnotherapy session doesn't "feel" like a hypnotherapy session.

Don't be disappointed if your first experience with hypnosis is not as intense as you may have expected. The more you *try* the techniques outlined in this book, the deeper your experience will become – in time.

During hypnosis, it is unlikely that you will fall asleep during the active hypnotic state.

You may feel completely relaxed (to the point that you feel light) but your senses, instead of becoming dulled and muddled during the hypnotic session, will actually be *heightened*. This heightening is necessary for the implanting of hypnotic suggestions.

The Nature of Hypnotic Suggestion

Hypnotic suggestions are used to create the desired changes to a person's way of thinking. There are four types of hypnotic suggestion:

1. **Verbal suggestions** – these suggestions are composed *purely* of sounds (words, music, etc.).

2. **Non-verbal suggestions** – these suggestions are the direct opposite of verbal suggestions. Non-verbal suggestions are composed *purely* of movements or gestures from the guide or hypnotherapist. Facial expressions can also be used to impart non-verbal suggestions to the person who is being hypnotized.

3. **Intra-verbal suggestions** – these suggestions are made up *specifically* of words.

4. **Extra-verbal suggestions** – these are hypnotic suggestions that are created with a combination of intra-verbal suggestion and non-verbal suggestion. This is considered the most effective and most powerful type of hypnotic suggestion.

Hypnotic Suggestibility

Suggestibility, on the other hand, refers to a person's *degree of compliance* to hypnotic suggestion without the interference of one's waking consciousness or logical consciousness.

In time, a person's *suggestibility* to specific hypnotic suggestions *increases* because existing ideas, beliefs or concepts are being automatically suspended during a hypnosis session. When a person is constantly given a particular hypnotic suggestion by a guide and a good rapport is established between the subject and the guide, *hyper-suggestibility* results.

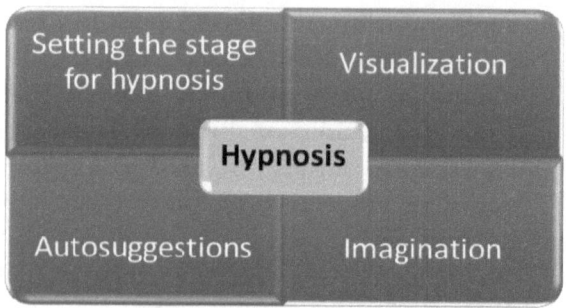

The four main tools of effective hypnosis

The Six Governing Principles of Hypnosis

As with every technique, hypnosis has its own governing principles or core concepts that are the basis of all hypnosis techniques:

1. **Thoughts have a direct effect on the body; the body responds readily to individual thoughts.**

Among all the known disciplines, hypnosis is one of the staunch defenders of the mind-body connection.

Hypnosis operates on the *fact* that the mind is much more powerful than one may have thought – so powerful in fact, that specific thought patterns produce actual physical reactions. No intervention or change can be produced without altering harmful thinking patterns.

For example, if a person has poor immunity and is greatly affected by chronic stress, he must change the way he *thinks* about his daily life before he can manage stress more efficiently. These changes are called *adaptations*. Negative ideas or thoughts must be transformed to *positive* ones with the help of hypnosis.

2. Whatever a person imagines to happen has a tendency to become actual reality.

When a person imagines something (*e.g.* getting a new job, finding new romantic love, etc.) the human subconscious isn't just producing random images or ideas. It is actually *setting goals*.

So if a person *expects* to get something in the near future, the subconscious half of the mind prepares the *waking consciousness* to make these subconscious goals a reality.

To make something manifest, a person's waking consciousness actively seeks to create the *proper setting* to make the goal materialize. In a nutshell, if you expect positive things to happen in your life, positive things will come.

3. Conscious striving *against* an existing habit or idea will produce a reversed effect.

This is called *the principle of reversed effect,* and here's how it works: when there is conflict between a person's natural willpower (which stems from his waking consciousness) and his subconscious goals, the harder he *strives* to accomplish a particular task, the higher his chances of ultimately failing.

A good example of this would be situations when we try to remember something *immediately* when the need for the long-unused information arises. Say you see a classmate from kindergarten on the street.

The other person recognizes you, waves at you and calls your name. In return, you panic and you try desperately to recall the other person's name.

You continue to struggle with recalling the information, but the name doesn't come. After the person has left and you have relaxed, the information you need suddenly comes to you — after the immediate need for it has passed.

4. Visualization is the key to habit-creation

The nervous system is in charge of continuing existing practices or habits. But it *does not* recognize the difference between events that take place in one's subconscious (imagination) and the real world.

That's why it is possible to use the power of creative visualization to change old habits or create more positive habits to replace old ones. By just *imagining* yourself performing new habits, you should be able to remove existing ones more easily than just *telling* yourself that you need to perpetuate a new routine or habit.

5. Autosuggestions make it easier for people to create new thought patterns and accept new ideas and goals.

Autosuggestions are words, symbols or gestures that represent ideas or sentiments with high emotional value.

Once a particular symbol, word, or gesture has been *associated* with an important idea, that *autosuggestion* alone should elicit a *physical response* from the body. Autosuggestions become even more powerful and effective if repeated over a period of time.

6. The emotional value of a suggestion is important.

When a hypnotic suggestion is made in such a way that the subject feels an emotional connection to that particular suggestion, then the suggestion has more impact.

Since existing habits and thought patterns are also formed with the "emotion + suggestion formula", the hypnotic suggestion will gradually replace existing patterns of thought in the subconscious.

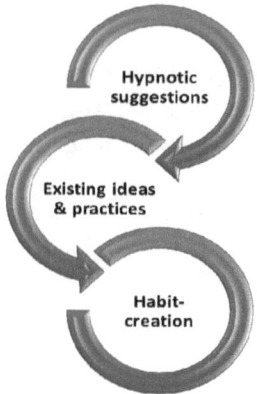

How habit creation becomes possible with hypnosis techniques.

Handling Resistance to Hypnotic Techniques

There's always a possibility that there might be subconscious resistance to hypnosis the first time you try it at home. This is normal since there is usually underlying doubt or fear of the hypnotic experience.

The idea of going into a hypnotic trance and being given hypnotic suggestion and autosuggestions can make *anyone* nervous – especially if their knowledge of hypnosis is limited to what popular culture has to offer.

The first step to reducing anxiety about hypnosis is to learn more about the discipline itself to gain familiarity. This familiarity with the method will also reduce the subconscious resistance to hypnosis, which ultimately affects the final outcome of hypnosis.

Do not be mistaken, though – it could take more than two or three hypnosis sessions to see major changes in your life.

The subconscious mind may be more willing to accept new ideas and life changes, but it is still affected by the constraints put forth by the waking consciousness. In time, the natural ability of the subconscious to accept repetitive suggestions as *true* will help the subject achieve whatever goals he has set for himself.

Remember, change is always a process. It does not happen overnight or instantly. If you are planning to enter into a hypnotic trance, drop a few suggestions, and expect some major results the next day, you're in for a big disappointment. Hypnosis does not work this way.

To improve your chances of success, you must also condition your subconscious to start accepting new ideas more frequently. You should start with small changes. As your subconscious mind becomes more accustomed to the small changes introduced through hypnosis, it will become more open to *major changes* over time.

Hypnosis *is* therapy – and therapy requires continuity in order to work. So don't forget to work on your goals a little bit *every day* to ensure success. It will not work if you do it once and forget all about the hypnotic suggestion after that one session.

In Focus: The Subconscious Defense System

While it might seem that the subconscious half of the human mind is very simple in its structure, it still has a *defense system* or mechanism of resistance that we have to contend with.

In adulthood, this subconscious defense system is at its strongest because the mind has had more time to absorb ideologies, norms and societal values. Ideas of what is normal and acceptable become even more dominant in the subconscious during adulthood.

So how exactly does this defense system work? Let's imagine that the human mind has an "input" funnel that has two pipes: one is directly connected to the subconscious (let's call this the "Input" pipe) while the other one leads *away* from the mind (let's call this the "Reject" pipe).

Now, visualize a stream of ideas coming in. Some of these ideas have no trouble passing through the "Input" pipe, but some ideas are diverted to the "Reject" pipe and never make it to the human mind.

Essentially, this is what happens to new or foreign ideas that seem to be too dangerous to even be considered. Through continuous conditioning, the mind becomes very selective as to what particular ideas should make it through the defense system.

Eventually, only a select group of ideas are considered "realistic" and "acceptable." When a person becomes fully convinced that there is only one "real" world-view, then the process of implanting new suggestions in the subconscious becomes more difficult. Difficult – but not impossible.

So why does the subconscious deflect new or foreign ideas in the beginning? Well, we can link this tendency of the human mind to distrust anything new to our most basic survival instincts. Imagine yourself living in prehistoric times.

There are only a few items that can serve as food and the rest of the available flora is usually toxic when consumed. The same applies to general environmental circumstances.

When something changes in the immediate environment that usually means danger. Eventually, *change* became synonymous with *danger*. This instinct has allowed humans to overcome the worst of circumstances for thousands of years (sticking to the old, avoiding the new, etc.).

The Three Gates

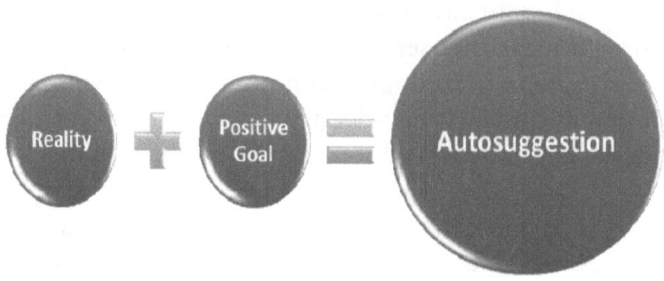

The formula to a successful and effective autosuggestion

This instinct may have served its purpose, but for hypnosis, these barriers make the technique less effective.

Now, in order to get past the subconscious defense system, one must be aware of the three major filters that prevent new ideas from being processed properly by the subconscious:

1. **Logical thinking** – By logic, we refer to any type of thinking that involves endless rationalization. Logical thinking is based on specific presuppositions, which makes it difficult for new ideas to make it through both the waking consciousness and the subconscious.

   One's own logical thinking is *unique* – it does not necessarily mean that what is logical for one person will be logical to another person.

It all depends on how a person has been conditioned to think.

2. **Emotions** – When an idea or concept is perceived as something that may cause humiliation, sadness, anger or grief, that idea is rejected by the mind. When such an idea arrives on the shores of the human mind, it is blocked by *existing* ideas that directly counter the logic of the new idea.

3. **Ethics** – A person's ethical values also block information or ideas that go against specific rules about how a person should think, act and feel.

   For example, it is possible that a person who was brought up in a predominantly Christian background would feel that reading and applying techniques found in a book on witchcraft is disagreeable or even unthinkable.

By using hypnotic suggestions that *resonate* or agree with existing ideas, the subconscious defense system can be bypassed through numerous hypnosis sessions.

That's why it is so important to craft your hypnotic suggestions carefully – and why statements should be focused *and positive*. Here are some easy tips to increase the effectiveness of any autosuggestion that you may want to add to a hypnosis script:

1. Use complete sentences that imply faith on your part on a certain outcome or goal. The most important component of these sentences is the *certainty* with which you say what you believe in, even if this outcome has not yet manifested in physical reality.

2. It would be best to construct autosuggestions that have a clear goal in sight. A good formula would be: *existing reality + positive goal = autosuggestion.*

3. Hypnotic suggestions and autosuggestions should always refer to the present time. Goals, on the other hand, should always be situated in the near future – and the hypnotic suggestion must create full conviction that although the end result of the effort has not yet been manifested, the desired outcome is just around the corner.

The following are examples of positive autosuggestions that anyone can use:

1. *I am becoming more aware of my true purpose in life, day by day.*

2. *Every day I feel that I am becoming more purposeful in what I do.*

3. *Every day I feel that my direction in life is becoming clearer and clearer.*

4. *My career is gradually becoming more and more rewarding, because I work hard and I focus on results.*

5. *I am falling in love with the world of man, all over again.*

6. *Right now I will start making my life better than ever.*

7. *I am fully capable of making positive changes to the world.*

8. *I will be contributing something meaningful and positive to the world today.*

9. *I believe that I am making other people's lives more meaningful and happier with the work I do.*

10. *I believe that people truly love me for what I am, and they appreciate me more day by day.*

11. *I am learning to be more giving to those who matter to me.*

12. *I am no longer afraid of problems at home and in my workplace because I believe that these problems are simply stepping stones to a bigger and better me.*

13. *I am now more aware and more responsible with my time.*

14. *Every day I am coming closer and closer to the weight that I have always dreamed of.*

15. *I have become more responsible with my own life and I am happy with my decision to be responsible in the first place.*

16. *I am finding it less difficult to find my place in the world.*

Chapter 6

The Basics of Creating Hypnotic Suggestions

We will be providing hypnotic exercises in the second part of the book. You are quite free to try one or all of the hypnotic exercises; however, this does not mean that you should not try formulating your *own hypnotic suggestions.*

No other hypnotic suggestion is more powerful than the one crafted by the subject – because you can be sure that your own hypnotic formulations will have enough emotional content to trigger changes in your behavior, thinking, etc.

Here are some essential guidelines in creating effective and lasting hypnotic suggestions:

1. Hypnotic suggestions are more effective if they are worded *positively.* Positive statements also ground the subconscious in the present, which facilitates the hypnotic process. So instead of saying, *"I will not smoke,"* a better formulation would be *"I am slowly letting go of my tobacco habit, day by day."*

2. Repetition is necessary during hypnosis; however, you should completely avoid terms like "you can do it!" or "you have it in you!"

These clichés have *no place* in hypnosis. When creating hypnotic suggestions, it is necessary to make the suggestions *personal* to make the maximum impact. The suggestions are meaningful to you, and you alone.

3. Suggestions should be crafted in the *first person* to be more effective. Each suggestion should also focus on a specific goal. If you have ten goals, you should have ten distinct, personalized suggestions for each goal that you wish to attain.

   So instead of saying *"You are not craving chocolate, sweets and junk food"*, it would be better to say, *"I am steadily losing interest in eating food with excessive sugar."*

4. Quantified hypnotic suggestions are a must - especially if you are dealing with issues like losing weight or building wealth. Here are some examples:

   a. *"I am steadily building my personal fortune to $100,000 in the coming months."*

   b. *"I am experiencing gradual weight loss each day so I can lose fifty pounds this year alone."*

   Again, it would be best to avoid short statements like *"I will be rich"* or *"I will lose a lot of fat."*

5. As we mentioned earlier, hypnotic suggestions are best when they are simple, direct, and given *in the present tense*. Doing this ensures that subconscious barriers will not interfere too much in the implanting of the hypnotic suggestions in the subconscious mind.

6. Use creative visualization whenever possible. Use your natural creativity and your boundless imagination to conjure images and ideas that would appeal to you *emotionally*. Adding emotions are the key to success – the more emotionally charged a hypnotic suggestion is, the more likely it is that you will respond quickly to it.

Creating the Perfect Environment for Self-Hypnosis

You're free to experiment with different environments when applying self-hypnosis techniques - but *make sure* that you *never* use hypnosis tapes and recordings when you are operating machinery or when you are out driving. Since you will be inducing a hypnotic trance, it would be best if you do hypnosis *at home* where you're safe from any accidents.

The room where you will be holding your self-hypnosis sessions should be a bit warmer than what you are used to (the extra bit of warmth will facilitate the hypnosis, since you will be more alert when it's warmer).

The air in the room should be clean and free from potentially distracting smells. As for your position during the hypnosis, it would be best if you used a *reclining chair.* You can recline during the hypnosis, but your arms should be placed at your sides to increase focus and discourage sleeping during the session.

If possible, place both feet on the ground (keep them flat and steady) and do not cross your legs during the session. Maintain a straight and firm posture during the hypnosis session to facilitate hyperawareness and to enter the hypnotic trance more easily.

During your first attempts at self-hypnosis, your hypnosis recordings should be played for at least twenty minutes *per session.* If you can have two or more hypnosis sessions throughout the day, that would be great – repetition gradually raises anyone's success rate as long as the sessions are done properly.

Notes on Using Your Own Hypnosis Tapes

Since you will eventually be creating your own hypnosis tapes to focus on different issues affecting your life, here are some easy tips to maximize the effectiveness of your self-hypnosis sessions:

1. If you can only listen to your hypnosis tapes during midday or evening, then stick to these times. This is part of the mental conditioning necessary to make the repetitive hypnosis work.

    Building a routine would also make self-hypnosis more *convenient* for you, because you won't have to sacrifice time for other things to give a bit of time for self-hypnosis.

2. Avoid lying down during hypnosis sessions – you might fall asleep!

3. Some people prefer making "bedtime hypnosis tapes". If this is your preference, by all means, pursue it. But instead of adding a section to the recording that actually wakes you up from the hypnotic trance, simply add a suggestion that will allow you to sleep immediately after the hypnosis session.

    Do not be overly concerned if you feel bored or tired when listening to hypnosis tapes. Because as long as you are hearing the hypnosis tapes, your subconscious will be absorbing and processing the positive suggestions contained in the recording.

    There will also be times that you feel that you have instantly forgotten what you have just heard. This is actually a *good sign* because this signals that your conscious mind has entered a deep level of hypnotic trance and it was unable to analyze the input.

4. A hypnosis recording can be as long as thirty minutes and can contain many hypnotic suggestions and affirmations. Each set of hypnotic suggestions is called a *section.*

    So if you have five groups of affirmations or suggestions, you have five separate sections.

    It is highly recommended that you add some music in between the sections of the recording. The additional music will help you focus, help keep you in trance, and also help deflect any distracting stimuli from the external environment.

5. There are no special requirements when it comes to who will read and narrate the contents of a hypnosis recording. As long as the person can read clearly, he can be assigned the task of reading through an entire hypnosis script.

6. Excessive effort on the part of the subject to enter a hypnotic trance is counter-productive. *Ease* into the trance – don't force yourself to accept hypnotic suggestions.

7. Avoid creating hypnotic suggestions that sound domineering – these will most likely be rejected by your subconscious.

8. Your motivation level has a large bearing on how effective self-hypnosis can be.

9. Instead of working on multiple issues at a time, focus on just one problem you are currently facing and work on that every day. When you have resolved that problem, move on to the next.

Progressive Muscle Relaxation

The mind-body connection is one of the most important guiding principles of self-hypnosis. That's why *before* any induction to a hypnotic trance, the body must be relaxed through a series of short exercises.

The following steps will help you perform *progressive muscle relaxation,* which will not only relax your body but will also help relieve tension and stress, and will ultimately calm your mind as well:

1. Lie on a couch or bed. Make sure that your back is completely flat. Straighten your arms and legs and just fall into a comfortable, natural lying position.

2. Clench your right hand for twenty seconds. Note the tense muscles in your right hand all the way to your right shoulder.

   Release the tension after twenty seconds and compare the feeling after you've released the clenched fist. Make sure that you take a deep breath before releasing your right hand. As you exhale, allow all the muscles in your right arm to relax.

3. Now clench your *left hand*. Repeat step # 2.

4. Next, let's work on your leg muscles. Start with your right leg – straighten your leg and use your right heel to press against the material beneath it.
    Hold this position for twenty seconds and release. Compare the feeling you get after releasing the tension to the sensation of having all the muscles in your right leg contract all at once.

5. Repeat step # 4 on your left leg.

6. The next area is the calf region of your legs. Once again, begin with your right leg. Point your feet and curl all your toes so that the underside of your leg will feel some pull/tension. Hold this position for twenty seconds. Repeat with the left leg.

7. The last region is near the shin bone. What do is simply point your feet and curl all your toes *upward* instead of downward. This will produce muscular tension on your shin region. Hold for the twenty seconds and repeat this step with the other leg.

8. Moving upward, it's time to relax the abdominal region. Pull the muscles in your

abdominal region *inward* and hold this position for just ten seconds. Release.

9. Squeeze your gluteal muscles (buttocks) together and hold for ten seconds. Release.

10. Move your head up as far as you can go so that the neck muscles become tensed. Hold for ten seconds and release.

11. Point your chin *downward* so that the muscles at the back of the neck become tense. Hold for a few seconds and release.

12. Your facial muscles should also be relaxed. Make different facial expressions to exercise each muscle group in the facial region. Hold for a few seconds each time you do and release.

Part 2:

Hypnosis Scripts

Chapter 7

Self-Hypnosis Scripts

After a few sessions, the "you" in any hypnosis script you are using should be replaced with "I", as this will constitute your advanced hypnotic conditioning.

For now, it would be best to begin with scripts that address the listener directly, as it has been found that for those who are just starting hypnosis, an external guide is more effective. The external guide is personified by the voice directly addressing the subject with the pronoun "you".

Hypnosis Script #1:

Basic Induction with Eyes Closed

The following hypnosis script was designed to bring you to a state of complete relaxation *with your eyes closed*. Before recording this script, it is necessary to write *hypnotic suggestions* using the guidelines we have set forth in the first part of the book.

These hypnotic suggestions can be inserted into any part of the script after the first few paragraphs (after the cue for hypnotic suggestions). Pay close attention to any pauses in the script, as these pauses mean you have to stop narrating the script for three to five seconds.

Start Induction

Relax where you are seated, whether it is a recliner or a chair. As you slowly become more comfortable with your choice of seating, you are also becoming more and more relaxed. You will feel as if you are falling deeper and deeper into a very relaxed state. **(Pause)**

Today, you will experience complete relaxation of your mind and body. **(Pause)**

Now close your eyes. Make sure that the light from the room is completely blocked out. **(Pause)**

As you close your eyes, you will feel more and more relaxed. **(Pause)**

Take three deep, rhythmic breaths right now. **(Pause)** When you inhale, let your chest fill with pure air.

Keep your chest muscles relaxed and let your diaphragm do all the work. **(Pause)**

As you exhale, allow all the negativity, hurt and stress to flow away. **(Pause)**

As you continue to breathe in this manner, you will feel light, relaxed and happy. **(Pause)**

Now take a single breath, and allow your chest to expand to full capacity. Hold the breath in for just a few seconds. **(Pause)** Slowly exhale.

All the pains, worries and stress that you have been holding in will leave with every exhalation. **(Pause)**

Breathe in again and hold it one moment. **(Pause)**

Slowly exhale. Feel your mental and physical tensions melting away. **(Pause)**

Take another breath and feel your lungs become full with life-giving air. Hold it one moment. **(Pause)**

Exhale – your lungs are working hard to dispel the harmful stress from your body. **(Pause)**

Do not worry about work or your chores. Nothing in this world can come between you and your relaxation. **(Pause)**

You are very, very relaxed. But your mind is still sharp and you are very alert. Your body is in a state of perfect relaxation as if you were in the most restful sleep. **(Pause)**

Your muscles, all tense before, are gradually becoming more and more loose, allowing you to simply relax. **(Pause)**

Every muscle in your face, neck, back, arms and legs are becoming relaxed. There is no need to worry or fret now. **(Pause)**

You have achieved a state of complete relaxation. Your mind is as clear and sharp as ever. Your mind is now focused on these suggestions. **(Pause)**

(Read hypnotic suggestions now)

Let go of any thoughts now and imagine yourself standing in a clean meadow. It is nighttime and the night sky is filled with endless stars. **(Pause)**

If you prefer, you can imagine the sky to be blissfully blank, as if a celestial hand was waiting to draw something across the night sky **(Pause)**

Whatever night sky you visualize, it is correct and it is *yours*. **(Pause)**

Now turn your attention to the very center of the night sky that you have visualized.

Imagine a large wheel just floating there. **(Pause)**

It doesn't matter what type of wheel it is – you can turn it into a bicycle wheel or perhaps the wheel of a car. Whatever you imagine it to be, the wheel becomes yours and yours alone. **(Pause)**

When you imagine the wheel in your night sky, picture that it is finally moving, turning slowly clockwise. **(Pause)**

As the wheel begins to turn endlessly, feel yourself entering a relaxed, hypnotic state. **(Pause)**

Your body is fully relaxed and you feel good. Your mind is as alert as ever. **(Pause)**

Every breath that you take brings you deeper and deeper into a state of perfect relaxation. **(Pause)**

It's time to let go of all the images that you have just created. First make the wheel disappear and then the night sky. You are preparing to depart from this wonderful and very relaxing state. **(Pause)**

In a few moments, I will begin counting backwards from five. When I reach one, you will fully emerge from your relaxed state **(Pause)**

5... 4... 3... 2... 1 **(Pause)**

If you are ready to sleep right now, simply turn off this recording and sleep soundly. **(Pause)**

If you need to do other things after this recording, you will emerge refreshed and ready for your day ahead. **(Pause)**

You will have extra energy for all your work and chores, and you will not become stressed because of these temporary things. **(Pause)**

At night, you will lie in bed and you will be able to sleep soundly and very restfully. No worries, no anxiety. Just peaceful, wonderful sleep. **(Pause)**

End Induction

Chapter 8

Hypnosis Script #2:
Basic Induction with Eyes Open

Start Induction

Find a comfortable place to sit in a quiet room. Place your hands at your sides and keep them relaxed. Take three slow and deep breaths. Focus on making deep breaths that will bring in pure, life-giving air. **(Pause)**

Every time you exhale, feel all the tension in your mind and body leaving. **(Pause)**

Now focus on a particular spot on the wall. Give your full attention to this spot. **(Pause)**

As you look at this spot, take a deep, nourishing breath and feel the air moving into your lungs. **(Pause)**

As you continue breathing deeply, your body is becoming more and more relaxed. **(Pause)**

As your body enters a state of pure relaxation, you can feel your eyes becoming heavier and heavier. **(Pause)**

Your mind and your body are both going into a very relaxing state of calm, quiet and pure relaxation. **(Pause)**

You are relaxed. Your mind is alert and you are very aware of every word and every sound that may come. **(Pause)**

Every deep breath that you take allows you to go even deeper into a state of relaxation. **(Pause)**

Every sound that you may hear as I talk will also allow you to sink deeper into relaxation. **(Pause)**

Nothing in this world can disturb you from what you are doing, which is simply resting and relaxing. **(Pause)**

Every worry and trouble that you have, all those things are gone now. **(Pause)**

Because you can think about them any time you want, but not now. **(Pause)**

You feel happy and light because you can discard these negative thoughts any time you wish. **(Pause)**

Your body and mind are both relaxed and you feel healthy, rested and ready for anything. **(Pause)**

Your mind is alert and ready. **(Pause)** Your mind is now focused on the following:

(Read hypnotic suggestions now)

Now allow your eyes to feel very heavy and very tired. Slowly ease your eyelids down so that all light is completely blocked out. **(Pause)**

By closing your eyes, you will be able to feel even more rested and more relaxed than ever. **(Pause)**

Imagine that you have an eye on the top of your head, and that you can see clearly with this eye. **(Pause)**

Visualize a place of happiness and serenity - your own personal paradise. **(Pause)**

Imagine yourself sitting right in the middle of this personal paradise of your own. **(Pause)**

You are comfortable, relaxed and happy where you are sitting. **(Pause)**

Not a thing in the world can disturb your peace and serenity now. **(Pause)**

Now in your state of complete relaxation, I will begin counting from three. As I count from three, every deep breath that you take will make you even more relaxed. **(Pause)**

As you exhale, allow yourself to become even more rested and refreshed. **(Pause)**

3... 2... 1 **(Pause)**

Every breath that you take will be better and even more relaxing than your last, long breath. **(Pause)**

Whenever you listen to this recording, everything will become easier and more relaxed than before. **(Pause)**

Your mind will always be alert and sharp whenever you listen to this tape. **(Pause)**

After listening to this tape, you will feel that everything that you want in life is just within reach, just ready for the taking. **(Pause)**

Nothing is too challenging, nothing is too difficult for a Superman (or Superwoman) like you. **(Pause)**

When it's time to rest at night, you will no longer have trouble falling asleep. **(Pause)**

You take naps whenever you want to and your worries and anxieties will no longer bother you. **(Pause)**

Your life is always improving and things are falling into their proper places all the time. **(Pause)**

Every day brings more joys and there is always something to be happy about. **(Pause)**

Every day you are improving within yourself. **(Pause)**

You feel really, really good right now. **(Pause)**

There is nothing in this world that can ruin your feeling of peace and relaxation. **(Pause)**

Focus now as I count backwards from five. **(Pause)**

When I reach one, you will awake from this great experience and your mind will be as alert as it will ever be. **(Pause)**

5... 4... 3... 2... 1.... **(Pause)**

You are now awake and you are ready for your day ahead. **(Pause)**

If you need to sleep after listening to this recording you can simply turn off the audio player and go to sleep. **(Pause)**

You will feel wonderfully refreshed after you sleep, every day. **(Pause)**

End Induction

Chapter 9

Hypnosis Script #3:
Conquering Procrastination

You are free to add any additional segments to this script, if you wish. However, you must limit the additional segments to general relaxation exercises, since every script must deal with only one specific issue that you would like to address with the help of self-hypnosis.

The structure of the following script can be used to create other scripts that deal with personal growth issues.

Start Induction

You have always been a natural leader, a persistent worker, and a very ambitious individual. **(Pause)**

You always want to tackle projects and tasks head on because you like adding to your list of daily accomplishments. **(Pause)**

There are many demands in your personal life and your career. **(Pause)**

You are relentless in accomplishing all the requirements of your life because you know you are making a difference and you are making things better not just for yourself but for everyone around you. **(Pause)**

You are an empowering force and you inspire those around you with your efficiency and your work ethic. **(Pause)**

You have the best type of personal discipline. **(Pause)**

You are able to accomplish everything that you need to do without sacrificing time for yourself and time for those who matter to you. **(Pause)**

It's not a question of your work or them, it's always *what can I do for both?* **(Pause)**

All your goals will be accomplished in no time because that's how you really work. **(Pause)**

Every day that passes after listening to this recording you will become more and more capable of handling long lists of things to do. **(Pause)**

It will not matter if you have to do things for your personal life or your professional life. **(Pause)**

You have the energy and willingness to accomplish all your goals for both with minimal stress and delay. **(Pause)**

You are no longer encumbered by large tasks that seem to have no start or finish. **(Pause)**

You are now able to analyze closely what needs to be done, step-by-step. **(Pause)**

Every large task has its parts, and you are able to see all these parts in their entirety and with extreme clarity. **(Pause)**

You are now able to work on individual parts of a task that compose the whole and you are very efficient in doing so. **(Pause)**

You have a clear set of values for work and you are sticking to your values no matter what situation comes. **(Pause)**

No matter how tough a situation, you always apply your sterling values to make things easier for yourself and those around you. **(Pause)**

Your alertness and awareness of things happening in your environment is always high - these never wane. **(Pause)**

When you are working, you are not encumbered by common distractions that prevent you from working ceaselessly. **(Pause)**

You are very capable of blocking out any or all distractions that will come to you whenever you are working on anything at home or at work. **(Pause)**

You will no longer be troubled by minor distractions because you are focused on accomplishing individual tasks. **(Pause)**

After each accomplishment, you are capable of resting and enjoying yourself. **(Pause)**

You are also capable of giving yourself the appropriate rewards for your accomplishments. **(Pause)**

You will not limit yourself to just work – you will know how to balance your work and your enjoyment, always. **(Pause)**

You are a natural born winner. **(Pause)**

You are a very talented person who knows his goals. **(Pause)**

You are the most focused person around when you are working hard on your tasks. **(Pause)**

You give high priority to your personal accomplishments because these are valued highly and are meaningful to everyone, not just yourself. **(Pause)**

After listening to this recording, you will bear the attitude and mentality of a born winner. **(Pause)**

You are independent, responsible, and you always have the confidence that you need for every situation in life. **(Pause)**

No matter what situation you face, you will use your winning attitude and your winning personality to overcome any and all challenges that you may come across. **(Pause)**

There is no problem too big and too challenging for a natural winner such as yourself. **(Pause)**

But you do not become complacent on your big list of accomplishments. **(Pause)**

You want to become better than yesterday, and better tomorrow. **(Pause)**

To do this, you must continue using your winning attitude and your self-reliance to accomplish tasks that are meaningful to your personal and professional life. **(Pause)**

You are the most determined person in the world. **(Pause)**

Your great determination allows you to conquer the most bleak of circumstances, so that you will still emerge as the victor in these challenging situations. **(Pause)**

You are capable of creating a winning self-image and you are capable of doing everything that you want to do, no matter how difficult each desire may be. **(Pause)**

What is important is that you do something to get what you want. **(Pause)**

And everything will fall into place once you start working on your goals. **(Pause)**

In addition to your self-determination, you also have high critical faculty. **(Pause)**

You are capable not only of intense focus on the tasks that you have at hand, but you are also capable of analyzing the various factors that will help you accomplish anything that you set your mind to. **(Pause)**

It doesn't matter if the goal is big or small. Whatever its difficulty or scope, you can handle it. **(Pause)**

Because you have the attitude of a true winner and you can always analyze the factors that will lead you to complete success. **(Pause)**

You are not afraid of changes and you are not afraid of taking responsibility for your life's toughest choices. **(Pause)**

Those choices are yours and the rewards from each decision are yours alone to cherish and enjoy. **(Pause)**

Every challenge that you surmount brings you closer to your biggest accomplishments in life. **(Pause)**

When you say something to yourself or to someone, you are always capable of following through with everything that you have said. **(Pause)**

When you promise that you will do something for work or for your personal life, you *will* accomplish what you have promised. **(Pause)**

Because you have the mindset of a determined, responsible and self-reliant winner. **(Pause)**

When you start something, everyone is sure that you will be able to finish whatever it is in no time. **(Pause)**

They expect nothing less of you because that is what you really are — a self-reliant and accomplished person who knows how to handle their responsibilities. **(Pause)**

You consider all your commitments sacred to you and you know how to follow through with each commitment because that is what you have always wanted to do. **(Pause)**

You are the person who says, "I will do that today!" whenever something has to be done. **(Pause)**

You like the idea of finishing tasks immediately so that you will have more time for yourself, your friends and your family. **(Pause)**

Your ability to finish tasks immediately will give you more freedom and more time to do all the things that you really want to do. **(Pause)**

In addition to your ability to do things immediately, you are also improving your ability to accomplish more and in very little time. **(Pause)**

You no longer needs hours upon hours of working time to get something done. **(Pause)**

You are a model of efficiency because you are able to break down the parts of a task so you can work efficiently and *quickly*. **(Pause)**

Now you are an expert in creating schedules when the going gets tough. **(Pause)**

Schedules make you happy and efficient because after a schedule has been accomplished, you are free to do other things. **(Pause)**

Things that bring you pleasure and enjoyment. **(Pause)**

Because personal accomplishments need to be rewarded. **(Pause)**

And you value diligent work above all else. **(Pause)**

You have now overcome the bindings of procrastination. **(Pause)**

End Induction

Chapter 10

Hypnosis Script #4:
Self-Confidence for Every Situation

You may add to the following script, but this script has a progressive relaxation phase at the beginning. You may extend the relaxation phase if you wish and you may add other hypnotic suggestions that relate to the issue of self-confidence.

Start Induction

Find a nice, comfortable position as you sit on an equally comfortable chair. **(Pause)**

Become aware of your posture and breathing. **(Pause)**

Feel the tension in your back slowly easing away from your muscles. **(Pause)**

Straighten your back and try to correct your posture as if you were arranging a stack of coins on a table. **(Pause)**

You are falling deeper and deeper into a state of increased relaxation. **(Pause)**

Now imagine any relaxing or wonderful place. **(Pause)**

It can be a meadow with a serene night sky or perhaps even a nice café in Paris. **(Pause)**

Whatever image you create, that image is the right image and it is yours. **(Pause)**

Now imagine yourself *in* the wonderful image that you have just visualized. **(Pause)**

Relax in your new surroundings and feel a nice, comforting breeze surround you in that wonderful place. **(Pause)**

Turn your attention to the sky. Whatever time of the day in your image, you will see the most beautiful and magnificent rainbow in the world. **(Pause)**

Observe the wonderful colors, each better than the last. **(Pause)**

You are becoming more and more relaxed as you appreciate the colors of the rainbow that has just manifested. **(Pause)**

As you focus on the new rainbow, you will realize that you are happy, content, and that everything that you have ever wanted was always within reach. **(Pause)**

You see that from this point on, you will always remember that anything that your heart may desire will be within reach. **(Pause)**

As long as the rainbow is there - which it always will be - you will be able to see ways to accomplish whatever you need to accomplish. **(Pause)**

You will be able to see the rainbow whenever you want to, and this rainbow is *yours* and no one else's. **(Pause)**

Whenever you feel anxiety, worry or fear of something, this rainbow will be there to accompany you and remind you that you are always the best, no matter how you may feel about yourself at certain points in your life. **(Pause)**

The rainbow signifies your winning spirit and your bright personality that will now shine through in any situation. **(Pause)**

Now look back to the wonderful image that you have just created. **(Pause)**

You are alone and you are relaxed, and you are free to do things here without the distractions of the mundane world. **(Pause)**

Think of what you would like to change in yourself to make things better for your life. **(Pause)**

Think of everything that you would like to improve, in whatever aspect of your life. **(Pause)**

Raise your eyes to the rainbow and say, "Now every goal that I have just set for myself will come true." **(Pause)**

Whatever you want to become in the present and in the future, you are now fully capable of accomplishing the little details to make your goals come true. **(Pause)**

There is nothing to stop you, and there has never been any obstacle to your success. **(Pause)**

The rainbow is a reminder that you will always be the true hero and winner in your own life's tale. **(Pause)**

Now that you have an image of yourself that you want to become, it's now time to make this a reality. **(Pause)**

Visualize entering a room that has a single television. There is a couch in front of the television. **(Pause)**

On the couch, there is a remote control. **(Pause)**

Take a seat in front of the television and turn it on with the remote control. **(Pause)**

The television will switch on but is still blank - it still needs one more thing to operate. **(Pause)**

Now comes the most important part. I want you to project the image of yourself that you have created a few moments ago *into* the screen of the television. **(Pause)**

Just imagine that your forehead is a projector and you are directly feeding the image of yourself to the television screen. **(Pause)**

The television screen lights up and receives your image. **(Pause)**

The television is operating in split-screen mode. **(Pause)**

On the right side of the television lies the image of your old self. It is very clear and very distinct.

All the features of your old self can be seen clearly from where you are sitting. **(Pause)**

On the other side of the split screen, you can see your *new* image being projected. **(Pause)**

But this new image is of lesser quality than the image of your old self. **(Pause)**

Imagine using the special remote control to alter the projected images on the television screen. **(Pause)**

As you fine-tune the projected image on the television screen, the old image of yourself will slowly become the muddled image and the *new* image will replace the old image. **(Pause)**

As you continue fine-tuning the split screen in front of you, the old image will be completely replaced by the new image. **(Pause)**

When the images in the split screen become completely alike, visualize the two images combining. **(Pause)**

As the images become unified on television, look at the rainbow once again. **(Pause)**

From this point on, the new image of yourself will become *your* ideal self, the one that you will strive to become, day by day. And you will succeed in doing so. **(Pause)**

Take a deep breath and a hold it a moment. Slowly exhale and feel all the tension leaving your body. **(Pause)**

Say "From now on, I am a changed person. I have the confidence to achieve everything I want in life. My self-confidence will increase day by day."

End of Trance

Chapter 11

Hypnosis Script #5:
Beat Anxiety

Anxiety comes in many forms. Whether you are suffering from occasional anxiety or from chronic anxiety attacks, this hypnosis script is for you.

This hypnosis script can also be used when you are tense or very stressed from work or from other responsibilities.

Begin Induction

As you listen to this recording, you are becoming more and more relaxed. **(Pause)**

Your heart will no longer race and your palms will no longer sweat uncontrollably. **(Pause)**

From this point going forward, you will always be calm because there is no need to be anxious or afraid of things that happen in your life. **(Pause)**

You will be able to do this because your mind is much more powerful than your emotions, and you are in charge of all your emotions, may they be positive emotions or negative emotions. **(Pause)**

With the same power of your own mind, you will be able to reach out and accomplish anything that your heart desires. **(Pause)**

This is what was meant to be. **(Pause)**

And you were not meant to feel worried, anxious or afraid beyond what is considered tolerable to any person. **(Pause)**

With the power of your own mind, you will be able to take firm hold of all your anxieties and you will be in control of these emotional and physical responses, and not the other way around. **(Pause)**

The words PEACE and RELAXATION will now signal to your mind and body that you will no longer succumb to anxiety in any of its forms. **(Pause)**

Whenever you think of the words PEACE and RELAXATION, all the tension in your mind and in your body will evaporate immediately. **(Pause)**

No level of anxiety will take over you, for as long as you think of the words PEACE and RELAXATION, your mind will automatically fight off anxiety, worries, fear and stress for you. **(Pause)**

Remember: PEACE and RELAXATION will be forever attainable, wherever you are. **(Pause)**

Take three deep breaths and with each slow breath, feel all your tensions melting away. **(Pause)**

Breathe in once and feel the negative emotions and anxieties leaving your body. **(Pause)**

Breathe once again, but this time, hold your breath and carefully exhale. **(Pause)**

You will feel more and more relaxed as you breathe. **(Pause)**

Nothing will disturb your PEACE and RELAXATION and you can always reach for calmness and tranquility wherever you are. **(Pause)**

Now imagine yourself outside, looking at the night sky. **(Pause)**

Visualize a newborn star, spinning and spinning clockwise. **(Pause)**

Imagine that you are able make the newborn star spin in place and as the star spins in the direction that you wish, you will become more and more relaxed. **(Pause)**

There are no worries, no anxieties. **(Pause)**

Just you and the star, slowly rotating the way you want it. **(Pause)**

You are in control and you feel fine. **(Pause)**

Your mind is alert but you feel very, very relaxed. **(Pause)**

Now, I want you to visualize a place of comfort and security. **(Pause)**

It doesn't matter if this place is purely of your imagination or if it's a real place that you find comforting. **(Pause)**

What is important is that when you are in this place, you feel secure and you no longer worry about the world at large. **(Pause)**

You can also think of your favorite time of the year when you visualize this special place of yours. **(Pause)**

Place yourself within this sanctuary and look around you. **(Pause)**

Try to make out the details of the place, even the smallest details, if you can. **(Pause)**

Try to find the wonderful smell of the air that has also made you comfortable and safe in this place. **(Pause**)

Think of how you feel when you are in this place and try to recall how tranquil and relaxed you are when you are away from the world, when you are simply alone and resting in this special place. **(Pause**)

Once you are able to recall how relaxed, peaceful and happy you are when you are in this special place, I want you to hold on to that feeling. **(Pause)**

Bathe in it, absorb every bit of it. **(Pause)**

Don't let it go; don't forget any part of the peaceful experience. **(Pause)**

Your mind is now focusing on the experience that you have in this chosen place and I want you to simply *prolong* the feeling. **(Pause)**

No worries, no fears. **(Pause)**

Just the feeling of happiness and peace that you get from being in this place. **(Pause)**

Perform this now.

(Insert peaceful music for at least 3 minutes)

Now, any time that you feel that anxiety is going to take over you, I want you to think of PEACE and RELAXATION to break the negative spell. **(Pause)**

I want you to always take control of this anxiety and vanquish it by going back to your special place where no hurt and worries can touch you. **(Pause)**

I want you to always recall how you feel in this special place so that whenever you are anxious about something, your happiness will take control of the negative emotions and vanquish it. **(Pause)**

You are very relaxed, and every muscle in your body is relaxed. **(Pause)**

Your eyes are getting heavier and heavier and yet your mind is always alert and sharp. **(Pause)**

Take three deep breaths and allow yourself to feel refreshed and energized. **(Pause)**

I will count from three, and when I reach one, you will awaken from this unique experience, no longer anxious or afraid. **(Pause)**

3... 2... 1... **(Pause)**

End Induction

Chapter 12

Hypnosis Script #6:
Vanquish Insomnia

Insomnia is often caused by extreme stress and tension. When a person is unable to manage his stress properly, the stress can cause sleep problems and even memory problems in the long term.

This hypnotic script was designed to bring a person into a progressive state of relaxation.

For best results, this script should be used as therapy for the person who is suffering from insomnia and should be played once before going to bed.

Unlike other hypnotic scripts, this particular script will require the subject to *lie in bed* to facilitate the therapy.

Start Induction

You are now entering a place where everything is peaceful and where anxiety and problems can never enter. **(Pause)**

Be in the most comfortable position as you lie relaxed in bed. **(Pause)**

Close your eyes gently and allow the peace and tranquility to take over your mind and body. **(Pause)**

Breathe deeply and fill your lungs with pure, life-giving air. **(Pause)**

Count to six before gently exhaling. **(Pause)**

Now take another deep breath. **(Pause)**

Now count to eight before gently exhaling. **(Pause)**

Feel your muscles becoming more and more relaxed as you go deeper and deeper into near-sleep **(Pause)**

Let your entire body fall back to the soft sheets and cushion **(Pause)**

Now we are going to progressively relax your entire body with some simple exercises. **(Pause)**

Extend your arms and clench your hands as if you are holding something that might fall at any minute. **(Pause)**

Hold for five seconds and let go. **(Pause)**

Feel the muscles in your arms and hands relaxing even more after you have released the pressure. **(Pause)**

Once again, extend your arms in front of you and clench your hands tightly. **(Pause)**

Hold for a few seconds and let go. **(Pause)**

You are becoming more and more relaxed and nothing can disturb you from your sleep. **(Pause)**

Your mind and body are resting quietly, untroubled by the outside world. **(Pause)**

Now let's move on to relaxing your lower body. **(Pause)**

Point your toes toward the end of the bed. **(Pause)**

Feel the muscles responding to the movement. **(Pause)**

Hold this position for a few seconds before letting go. **(Pause)**

Let your muscles relax and fall back gently to the bed. **(Pause)**

You are becoming more and more relaxed as you perform these exercises. **(Pause)**

After relaxing your legs, let your toes point toward your head, so that your leg muscles will again contract. **(Pause)**

Hold this position for a few seconds and let go. **(Pause)**

Let your leg once again fall back to the sheets. **(Pause)**

Now that you are relaxed and untroubled, you are going to make some positive changes in your subconscious mind. **(Pause)**

From this moment on, your subconscious mind will no longer interrupt your sleep, nor will it interfere with your relaxation before you are able to sleep. **(Pause)**

Your subconscious mind will be continually reconditioned as you breathe normally. **(Pause)**

You will only awake in the middle of the night if there is something truly urgent that requires your attention. **(Pause)**

Other than such rare situations, you will not be disturbed by anything. **(Pause)**

You will now feel very relaxed and very sleepy. Turn off the audio player and fall into a deep sleep.

End Induction

Chapter 13

Hypnosis Script #7:
Self-Image Improvement

A person's self-image has a large bearing on his self-confidence and his ability to socialize with different people.

The following hypnosis script focuses on making general improvements on a person's self-image.

If you wish, you can insert progressive relaxation phases in the recording to facilitate the hypnosis, or you can perform the progressive relaxation *before* playing the hypnosis recording.

Start Induction

Starting today, you will find that the average weight is the best possible weight for you. **(Pause)**

You will be more responsible with what you eat and you will no longer be interested in food that you know is not good for your weight and health. **(Pause)**

Through this, your body will naturally love the change and you will naturally lose weight. **(Pause)**

You are no longer bound by issues of self-image. **(Pause)**

You are beautiful inside and out and you believe this because this is the truth - it has always been the truth. **(Pause)**

Because of your inner strength you have everything you need already to fight any eating disorders. **(Pause)**

From now on, your self-image will always lean toward the positive and never the negative. **(Pause)**

You will do this because this is the truth – you are beautiful, and every day you are coming closer and closer to each and every goal that you have in life, not just your weight loss goals. **(Pause)**

You love who you are and you no longer hurt yourself because of how you look. **(Pause)**

Any issues that you have with your physical appearance will now be resolved through natural means. **(Pause)**

You will have the self-confidence to socialize and reach for everything that you want in life. **(Pause)**

Nothing is holding you back and nothing will ever hold you back ever again. **(Pause)**

Your reality is being created anew. **(Pause)**

Your new reality is full of hope and dreams that have already come true. **(Pause)**

End Induction

Chapter 14

Common Hypnosis Questions Answered

Modern hypnosis may be developing at a healthy pace, but that doesn't bring an end to the many misconceptions about the practice.

This section covers the most common questions that people have for professional hypnotists/hypnotherapists. If you ever decide to approach a professional hypnotherapist, at least you will have some knowledge of the common hypnotherapy practices that are presently being used.

Q: Why is a quiet place necessary for hypnosis? Why can't I do it when I'm eating at a restaurant or when I'm with friends?

A: While it is possible to copy a digital hypnosis recording into a portable media player and carry around the player with you, we do not recommend any hypnosis that takes place in crowded or noisy locations.

This is because you really need to be able to concentrate on the positive suggestions and instructions contained in the hypnosis recording. You will only be able to do this if you are in a quiet place, free from common distractions.

Q: Why is hypnotic induction needed during a hetero-hypnosis session?

A: When you have a formal guide or hypnotist, that person should be able to lead you through the different phases of hypnosis (*e.g.* relaxation, hypnosis proper, etc.) Induction is the formal starting point of hypnosis. Induction also prepares a person to accept the hypnotic suggestions that have been prepared.

Q: Why do some hypnotherapists ask their patients to perform deep breathing alongside muscle relaxation?

A: Deep breathing is one of the most effective methods used to relieve tension. Deep breathing also facilitates hyper-awareness.

Q: Why is the imagination so important to hypnosis?

A: The imagination is a distinct part of the human mind that is not completely reliant on the waking consciousness. In fact, the human imagination is richer and more vibrant when we are asleep – when the waking consciousness is temporarily suspended during dreaming.

Setting goals for yourself also requires the healthy use of the human imagination; because what we are focusing on when we do self-improvement sessions is to take the reality that you have now, and implant an ideal reality that you wish to attain in your subconscious. Now the only way that this ideal reality can be implanted is if it is creatively visualized through the imagination first.

Q: Are awakenings really necessary at the end of every hypnosis session?

A: Unless you are making a bedtime hypnosis recording, yes. You see, hypnosis has three main parts – induction, hypnosis proper, and the awakening.

During the induction phase of a hypnosis session, you are giving yourself a cue that you have to temporarily suspend your usual pattern of thinking (conscious thinking) to give way to the hypnotic suggestions.

Once the hypnosis session has been completed, the signal to awaken tells your mind to end the current trance and revert back to the line of thinking that you were using *before* the session began.

References

BOOKS:

Alman, Brian & Lambrou, Peter *Self-Hypnosis: The Complete Manual for Health and Self-Change* (USA:Bruzzel/Manzel, Inc.) 1983

Blair, Forbes Robbins *Instant Self Hypnosis: How to Hypnotize Yourself With Your Eyes Open* (Illinois:Sourcebooks, Inc.) 2004

Blair, Forbes Robbins Blair *Self-Hypnosis Revolution: The Amazingly Simple Way to Use Self Hypnosis to Change Your Life* (Illinois: Sourcebooks, Inc.) 2007

Bryants, Mike & Mabbutt, Peter *Self Hypnosis for Dummies* (England: John Wiley & Sons, Ltd.) 2010

Eastwood, Noel *The Self-Hypnosis Handbook* 2nd ed. (Australia: Herald W. Tietze Publishing Pty. Ltd.) 1995

Goldberg, Bruce *Self Hypnosis: Easy Ways to Hypnotize Your Problems Away* (New Jersey: New Page Books) 2006

Hewitt, William *Self Hypnosis for a Better Life* (Minnesota: Llewellyn Publications) 1997

Hogan, Kevin & LaBay, Mary *Through the Open Door: Secrets of Self-Hypnosis* (Louisiana, Pelican Publishing Company) 2000

Hunter, C. Roy *Master the Power of Self Hypnosis* (New York: Sterling Publishing Company) 1998

Karim, Shaid *Self Hypnosis in the Management of Stress and Anxiety* (England: Eyelevel Books) 2002

Kuhns, Bradley *The Wonderful World of Self-Hypnosis* (USA: B. Kuhns) 1988

Marsoleck, Patrick *Transform Yourself: A Self Hypnosis Manual* (Montana: Inner Working Resources, LLC) 2006

O'Briaian, Cathal *Powerful Mind Through Self-Hypnosis: A Practical Guide to Complete Self-Mastery* (UK: O-Books) 2010

Perkins, Wayne *How to Hypnotize Yourself Without Losing Your Mind* (USA: Trafford Publishing) 1947

Index